Tales Of A Stone Mason

A Book of Poetry

By

Ryan Fredric Steinbeck

Tales of a Stone Mason

Printed in the United States of America.

First Printing

ISBN: 978-0615773902

Acknowledgements And Thank You's:

Thanks to Cindy, for constant inspiration. Thanks to my family, friends, poets, musicians, and writers who continue to create and inspire.

Thanks to Cindy Steinbeck for the photo.

Thanks to Michael Steinbeck for the illustration and covers.

Table Of Contents:

Table Of Contents:

To The Reader:

I realize the money spent on this book could've been used to pay your monthly expenses. I just wanted to say that's not lost on me. Thank you for purchasing my book.

Ryan Steinbeck

Greater Than Love

After forty years of weakness
Watching the fall of this settlement
My ears have finally heard the call

I won't let my history
Color future canvases
These choices were revealed to me
As I shattered indestructible barriers
That constrained me for so long
It had nothing to do with freedom
There is no freedom without love

Sometimes earth, sky, and water
Appear to align and form an arrow
Pointing in the direction I should go
I'm only required to observe, then follow

With fear aside on the broken beach
Ripples are directed toward me
I recognize this was always taking shape
Before today I cowered and reviled potential

If abashed by one thousand lights and sounds
Still I can observe silence
I know I'm here to accept and comprehend
There is nothing greater than love

Begin To Understand

Passing the clock tower in the district
I am cast back 200 years
The reflection off the windows drawn in
The chill in the air is opportunely

The surfacing of this rebuild
Once longstanding
The feeling of anticipation unexplored
I am connecting to a center greater than one
A circuit of beginnings harnesses perimeters

I am restless, I wait for a call
I am balanced, I can feel what I want
I am guided by these ships
Carrying my soul to faraway lands
Before today I didn't know

The err of dissension
In the temples of absent hearts
Reveals to me I'm just beginning to understand
All the ways I can love

I've encompassed the fear that became me
Alluring it up to awareness
Forcing demolition and resolution
Constructing pyramids of gratitude over land
You are a gift, a true treasure
We collectively waited out the storm
Until I surrendered to all that I am
Could I begin to understand

Where I Am

Hands outstretched before me
I move through the bituminous setting
An impatient glimmering up ahead
I foretell a blinding by white

Born in the clothes I wear
Avoiding one big disaster
An epic beautiful mess
Throwing high hopes down wishing wells
Looking out to the distant shore
Where angels fear to tread

Hearts cast in plaster
Under floors in cement cellars
Freed by raging fires of assent
From the asylum's cocktail of despair

There is a great undoing before me
An uncluttering of clichéd lullabies
Before the sunsets sequence of homecomings
I appoint reliance of my own compass
Then I bridge chasms once perilous

Here there is something good
Where sovereignty once appeared impossible
There is semblance of an appropriate ending
It feels like a good place to start

I've been everywhere and nowhere
With knowledge of everything and nothing
Essentially I don't want anything
To infringe upon inaudible sounds

I proclaim intelligence and ignorance
Crying utopian grievances
Still there never is a time
That this isn't where I am

I Predict

I predict a quiet end to the years
Eventual ceasefire amid enemies
Prayers answered
Resolution

Love defined by action
True spirit of devotion
Absolving of differences

We'll arrive at Heaven's Gate
Knowing one another
Forgiving one another

Spending eternity with answers
Knowing we sought a pure heart
Working toward enlightenment
Finding peace

Fields & Streams

As I walk in the fields and alongside streams
Frantic crispness of morning air
Has me thinking
Violins of ripples catch my attention
The sun hasn't shown itself in a long while

The melting snow and ice are suggesting
Different times are ahead over the ridge
The rays focus their attention up there
I hurry my pace so I don't miss an opportunity

As I shake off the rust of the past
Branches shake off the cold harboring
Of a long overdue passing season
As if it's a collective conscious decision
Not to remain in the comfort of stagnation

I clench my fists
And feel the onset of urgency
Passing a town gathering off in the distance
I am alone in these steps I am taking
But I am not lonely

Sandstone castles can be seen from here
I wonder if they see me
And what they're thinking
I veer from the quiet comfort
Of the stream's music
As an incline begins
And wind forces its presence
These offering distractions
Won't prevent my focus

It's as if these polarizing effects
Are only offered as challenges
To see if I'll call their bluff
As I cross the line
That's all they appear to be

All behind me is gone but not forgotten
For with everything comes new challenges
As I lift my eyes to the warmth
I know I am ready

Submarine

These waters aren't as they seem
I don't recognize the man
In the family portrait
I've been forgiven except unto myself
As I dance with waves, direction, and hope

I don't put lives at risk if I don't have to
Don't fill the glass that can never get full
This flag never knew half mast
Until we learned conscience and took heed

Our journey laid waste to years behind
When our homebound ship arrived
We ask the bartender for another round
As we reminisce about what we tried to forget

This town likes to remember
Honoring the survived and fallen
We always show up, smile, and wave
But we never feel like celebrating

Over years we let our guard down
Old men in new clothes
Hearing and eyesight transformed
Into passing hours of unawareness

It wasn't until it was too late
Nothing left to look back on or regret
The impact immediate and widespread
Witnessed by those flying overhead

The comfort cradled us and made us weak
In the end it got the best of us
We all thought we had them beat
But they arrived by submarine

The Lessening

In the domain of senses
Conflict and sins are mended
Steadying breath is focused
Fixed on peace and stillness

There is no establishment
No form and no shape
I denounce any connection
From cultivations of benevolence

The turning and shifting
To a new way, a new light
An old compilation of myself
Lay before me in masses of memory

I accumulate articles of importance
Then set fire to the surplus
I unhook the chains of attachment
Then sever mental bondage

A wider canvas
With new dialogue
I step into fertile landscapes
I wade in streams of consciousness

Manifestations of historical thievery
Smashed to smithereens
By my heart's insurrection
I may not be firmly positioned or engaged
But the limitless firmament is before me

Reclamation

I'm a hybrid, a new innocent
I'm not far away
Though not as close as I'd imagined

I hear a whistle of a distant train
The rush of morning commute
The rumble of bass from a passing car
Engines idling as they wait to merge
All symbols of what we call freedom

We did what we could to escape
Only to fall into another trap
Not everyone can prosper, some must suffer
I've held the trophy in this interval
I hope to discard and diffuse this penalty

In frozen caves beyond waterfalls
Razors to the touch
I look for humanity among the inhumane
Become the institution I wanted to escape
Under a leader praising the heavens in light
Worshipping corruption in the dark

For a hardened mind
Refusing belief in rainbows
Only rain will be experienced
The loudest avalanche
From the quietest echo
There's always a means of escape
Behind walls and through pastures
I rise above
Standing on pillars to see the sun
I project myself into my own mercy
From a scheme plotted inside my head
I erase who I am to the outside world
As I become someone completely new

Kamakura Sunrise

Morning rain
On a day so deserving
Reflects the soul's mood

Truth shrouded
Fleeing into opaqueness
Hopeful empathy

Slow clearing
The sun's appearance
Karma is waiting

All the postscripts in my head are outdated
I'm waiting outside the sphere that surrounds your logic

Saint Chrisostom And The Untimely Exit, 1867

Days of life in Ulrich never changed
A slow dismantling mundane repetition
With blistered fingers, a mind full of ideas
I was constantly aspiring for enlightenment

The need to survive the darkness
To feed the mouths at the table
Neither patience nor perseverance
Were qualities rewarded with opportunity

I stayed true to my meaning
To honor my wife and my child
I wanted to do something my father never did
Before time got the best of me

Nothing could foresee or prevent
What misfortune was willing to allow
I was told the road ahead
Would give in to obscurity
That I should make my peace

Inevitability took hold
I caught a glimpse of this oblivion
I felt my soul preparing for a journey
I placed a wager on my confidence

I said a prayer for the next generation
Expecting to see an arsenal of ingenuity
That I could be proud of
I look down on a better time and place
With minds better equipped
I'm still waiting for the ending
Still hoping my dream will be fulfilled

Frank

The message you sent
You weren't good enough in your own skin
Spread like generational wild fires
Through minds that followed

Frank I didn't know you
Or your reasons why
All I see are results
Of your decisions

You walked the path of self-absorption
The beginning was haze and dust
Today it stretches continents
As it becomes irreversibly paved

One million excuses
Sent you on your way
Everything is in a name
Yet you opted for anonymity

Today we've rebuilt optimism
We believe we can clean up the chaos
There's a history of second beginnings
That became the origins of better days
Something we hope can be cyclical

Cherokee

Voices from asylums
Calling from past
We are dust
Muted to ground
With our heads bowed

The mind has been tamed
Trained like pets
Streamlined reactions
To a holocaust of rights and land
Decipher written word
To apply how they choose

Nestled in our beds
Dreaming of hope
Feeling the warm touch of change
While our world is burning outside

Relics of a forgotten way
Wax museums
Contents from clay
Pigeonholed to corners of state

Orphaned fathers and sons
From the keeper
The friendly enemy
We have been deceived
But we have survived

1993

Twenty years late
An open road still calls me
These organic, fundamental discoveries
Established a chain of inspiration

My foundations built on sound
Connected by a mind stoned in philosophy
A stage to reveal my blueprint
Across a mystical empire of disclosure

I thought I heard the earth's rotation
The chime altered once evident reverberations
New tools of existence
Postured untold theories
There was finally something I could adhere to

Tired of being suspended at the surface
I moved to hunt the depths
I found answers to be inadequate
When the derivation of blood is predetermined

With the assent of my immovable conscience
Locked doors now ceremoniously opening
Revealing a fraction of my whole
This year I recognized infinite potential

Wisconsin

The heart and veins of this republic
An armory of decomposed words
A bunker latent with consequences
A wasteland deficient in optimism

I watch and savor the gathering of shadows
A desire for affectation
Looms over deified ground
She is standing at the back of the world's lot
Deferring her inquiries of acceptance

The grind of steel on steel
A train's feeling of disquiet for a cold land
The farewells of runaway spirits
Halted the growth of these family ties

The old courthouse viewed in transience
Every intersecting road insinuates a union
Awareness of depth and disposition
Minutes between the thoughts of her
Transform from days into years

I recognize the boundary is imminent
I liken it to times bygone
I've been learning to keep pace
Even as wheels are persevering

Entering the forsaken valleys
With remnants of past echoes and dust
Serpents are curled in reserve
Poised to attack at first movement

Too much devastation and disjointed promise
Disseminated among the widespread wreckage
So long have these arctic fires been burning
No longer can they remain silent

Nobody's Son

I am becoming
I am the straw and the camel's back
I live inside my block of ice
Where the sun cannot reach

I am glacial
I am relentless
As I rescind my propaganda
Deny my affiliations

Mind your head
These wires hang low
Protecting the scarred heart
Unearthed from ruin
Left broken and abused

They are judge, jury, executioner
Eager to drop the charges
As long as I confess
But they abandoned me first

I wasn't strong enough
To start over in your company
There's nothing else I could've done
Nobody's son

Ancestry

We fall into what we don't quite understand
There are times when the curtains open
Shedding light on old knowledge
That is sometimes better left alone

He was born of kings
Ruling in parliament
An active participant
Ending hatred through peace

I was drawn from another thread
Born of cowards, liars, swindlers and violence
Abusing spouses, stealing from mothers
Changing a hereditary name to hide in fear

A lineage of permanent mediocrity
Haphazardly stumbling away from yesterday
Never having made a splash
Never hit the ground running

We said and did
What was better left unsaid and undone
Always convinced we are right
Even though our trails prove otherwise

We live for the last word
Achieving pleasure in conflict
Gratification in guilt
As the ship of fools expands

Although descent cannot be undone
It takes one courageous mind
To acknowledge existence of potential
To distinguish an alternate course
To welcome benevolent, impartial passengers

Burdens

Though this water I drink today
Is no longer cloudy nor subjective
Without it the trees will not grow

I carried my burdens in the dark
Nothing is as clear as daylight
The moment I realized I wasn't special
I let my burdens go

I raised the rates
Raised the stakes
Buried my hands into the soil
Until gratitude rushed out

Now I tell fables of an imposter
A man who inhabited this skin and these bones
He let kingdoms burn and love fall to ruin
Before he recognized what was lost

There is nothing left from you
Still everything has its origin
I kneel in the shade of the trees we planted
Thank you for giving me life

One hundred miles from here
I recall a conversation
That ended before it began

Fields Of Barren

A rising of exploration
From the beginnings of a river
Amid the fall of philosophic insurgence
Winding through the narrows of memoirs
As minds move into conception
The minutes are waiting in disorder

After a week of nights the sun will rise
Symmetries may change but resolve endures
Guiding light along the trail of one thought
Existing in the spaces between resentment
The search for my epilogue is folklore

The balance of rain seeps in conscience cracks
The drought signifies a harvest is ahead
Over these fields once barren
Flowers will begin to bloom

A Missed Opportunity

As the wheels went up
And your departure neared
I was dismissive
I missed my opportunity to tell you

Though you've painted many hills
Brought life to dark boulevards
At some point there's atrophy
Cracks in the walls can no longer be filled

Your message will resonate
Like the inspiration you shaped
You brought out the best in me
I am still learning from you

You will write beautiful music for heaven
Playing it the moment you arrive
It will echo from a loud speaker
In the hearts and minds of those who reminisce

For the rest of eternity
They will be joyful everyday
They will hear it all around and smile
They will know you made it safe and sound

Southern Rain

We were forced to pull off the road
That was what they meant by southern rain
There were no other moments than this
No gravity to hold us down

The sky opened up by Farm to Market 99
The sun pleaded its case to stay
I-37 to Corpus Christie
Just to say we did

Ocean Drive over Emerald Cove
On to Padre Island
The warmest water sent our invitation
From the center of the Gulf of Mexico

It was my mission to give you what you wanted
It was in my genetic code to fail you
I effectively separated the puzzle pieces
To reflect a happy ending

When I use the rearview mirror
I forgive these transgressions
Nobody was innocent or forthright
As we descended into deluges of words unsaid

I consider it a turning point
I owe you a bit of gratitude
Whenever I remember the Texas rain
I smile a little, then go on with my day

Cold Enough To Snow

The roofs and steeples
Covered before my childhood
Ahead of my eyes but never seen
It's always cold enough to snow

Snow fell across the alley
Snow fell on the universities
Snow fell on our wedding day
Burying the flowers we planted

They always forecast a change of seasons
But the wind tells a different story
A flag of truth or convenience
The icy air remains

An era of dead reckoning
Debridement of derivation
Escaping the effluxion
Of oppressive masquerades
That harbored me in middle distance

Constantly beginning, never ending
These transformations revise uncertain hearts
Fables of warming lands
From untraveled braggarts
Turn out to be broken promises

Radar Of Hope

Across the way there's a riverbed
She tills an empty garden nearby
Stirring up the atomic dust
Then rolling in the mud
To cover her lingering scent

Here in this half-standing temple
We are feasting on remnants
Taking bets on what collapses
The pride of hopeful survivors
Or the remaining church rafters

The kettle of vultures overhead
Display a hopeful pattern in their flight
We've learned to be present in ignorance
No more friends, enemies, or familiarity
Just everyone waiting patiently

In a world that was once too small
All the satellites are gone
You were my satellite
My radar of hope
But no more

Sally And The Windmills

Sally lived on the inside
She cried as she watched her parents fight
One day her father left in moonlight shadows
She marks this date by dancing in the park
Twirling as she kisses the sky

Relentless winds distracted sounds on that day
Of door slams and irrepressible cries
Eventually there was no solid ground
Only the scattered fragments of lost and found

This town would not tolerate a broken home
Furthermore the thoughts of the unfaithful
So the papers reported he fell to his death
From a windmill he had been assembling

The winds always change direction
Her thoughts carried easy on current
Ten years working in rain and snow
In duty to a troubled mother at home

In the beginning of the fall
Sally was held hostage without restraint
On the plateau of her own doing
Among the chattels of her own land

Soon it crawled underneath her skin
Emotions exploded like landmines
One day the her mother received a call
Sally wouldn't pick up the phone

She was a flower that refused to die
A mission of a journey inside
Thousands of miles later on the beach
She followed the coastline to her new life

She was the unsung hero and villain
Just as her father was before her
She set her lawn chair in front of her cabin
When she captured a powerfully weak resistance
Her memories exploded in rushing anger
As the face that left her as a child
Came into focus by her side in the sand

United by the same crime
The dialogue lost between them
Sitting in silence at sunset
As their journey together resumes
Unexpected and unpiloted

Stories From Mexico

A summer in the middle of nowhere
A convenience store where I stopped for fuel
The lights were off, no cashier
Just a man lying on a counter

He smelled of beer and cigarettes
I touched his hand as he opened his eyes
"I'm sorry, I was checking for a pulse"
"I tilled the fields, then hit the bar across the street," he said
I looked but there was no bar over there
"We're fellow travelers, you and I
You need to know
The gold world they pledged doesn't exist,
There's only aluminum"

"There are ghosts in the tumbleweeds
It rains but crops won't grow
Money goes out but never comes in
This is my last gasp of hope
Or I lift my praying eyes to the sky
And look for a way back home"

He winced a smile as he limped away
Somehow he was fantastically content
As if this was the expected consequence

I could only smile as I continued
The stranger's trivial world was vast
Turning resentment into joy
Believing that better times were ahead

The Harbor

Reverberations of wonder all around
Out of control on the wind
Raging in from her harbor
Shifting the damaged landscape

Building on passages
From ancient kings and heroes
These armies in resistance
Withdrawing their forces

The council of nobles
In confession with complacency
Merchants and craft workers
Losing control of their guilds

Scouring the royal parks and forests
I find no painting or sculpture
As beautiful as this vision
Assembled from homeward passage

As the moon begins low tide
On this wherry I trace likeness
Upstream the ancestries of this splendor
Castles decorated with gardens and flowers
Complicated outlines are simplified
I see the harbor that calls me
I've incessantly continued sculling
Every day it is my purpose

The Archaeologist

This archaeologist
Hoping for chronological unearthing
In the soil of contaminated lands

Asking the wrong questions
To collect the wrong answers
He struggles in appreciation of landscapes

Obsessed with his craft
Declaring the rejection of creature comforts
Focusing on pieces instead of the whole

Fearing erosion and run-off
That the skeletons he buried
Will rise to the surface

Like generations before
There's nothing underneath
So he digs for privatized artifacts

Living on conjecture and judgment
Fixated on the newest discoveries
As personal welfare corrodes around him

He could show true compassion and honesty
Or pretend to care about something else
But he can't excavate what fails to exist

The archaeologist calls to the wind
He mined the chasm too deep
Only echoes are left to reply

Calpe

Our minds and hands were positioned
We raised the moorings
Setting course for the strait of Gibraltar
Trespassing in Spanish waters

The captain cautioned our hopes
As we sailed through the calm
With food in short supply at home
We weren't worried about the in between
Despite the raging waters

Off in the distance the Moorish Castle
The familiar blue-grey shale
As a child I explored the caves
Before I was sent off to war

As I awoke from my daydream
I took account of the hurtling darkness
Soon transformed into driving rain
We surged through high shadows
As primitive fear took hold

Spreading tales of the disappeared
We fought and became divided
One side advised we should turn back
Weighing the odds of the night
Deciding the risk was too high

The captain did not recoil
He took a stand and bestowed directive
We would see this to the end
Whatever the end shall be

As he spoke with his back to the horizon
We observed the congregation of darkness
Unlike anything ever seen with these eyes
Maybe the violence that followed
Was nature's way of getting even
A plan to punish the guilty
On a ship with its fate predetermined

I don't remember the dawn
Nor accounting of the wreckage about the shore
My true and final elegy
Was a vision of my family
I will not have a legacy
Only a letter from the harbor
And a local namesake bar

Our spirits with our loved ones
They were always in our hearts
They will celebrate our courage
As we become one with fairy tales
Soon to be diminished by passing time

Diomede

Our blood ties
Without remaining language
Keeping our eyes on each other
While standing nations apart

These proposed treaties
Across international timelines
Denying rule of law
Misleading the mainland in the distance
A classified militant invasion

I bare no witness
To the result of this flood
To the hand that pulled me out
Or carried me to surrounding shallows

Your light was always dimming
I had no contrast until my eyes adjusted
At the periphery of this island
There was only one proper conclusion

Run

If your ship is sinking
Or the floorboards collapsing
If your days are numbered
But you're still not counting
The sky may be laughing
As the sun lights your way
Moving every muscle
Toward the same conclusion
A revision disguised as an ending
You refused to throw your hand
Nor give up the ghost
Not beleaguered by the sounds
That were once supporting voices
Eventually the subconscious takes over
And the pain will numb
The secret is in strategy
The story now elaborate and complex

It may have been impossible
But you continued to listen
You kept moving ahead
One day builds on the next
One foot in front of the other
Run

Today

Today is an unusually quiet day
The electricity spikes
Before the rolling dunes
Hinting this is about to change
As the busiest station waits ahead
I could sleep; it's been a trying year
Instead I try to feel important, connected.
Shedding my daily responsibilities
As I head for the city

Today I don't really have a purpose
I don't have a dialogue
Or vocabulary I wish to use
I would rather digest all that I've seen
Over the past several years
As I remain in silence much of the day
Around me the density of chatter increases
I hear a distant whistle of an oncoming train
The repetitive track turbulence
Takes time to transition
Into the hurried halting haze hidden up ahead

One voice speaks of drama this past Christmas
The weight of his conversation heavy
As it sinks to the aisle
Drowning in a puddle left by a footprint
Originating from the dampness of the earth
After last night's rain

Another voice carries optimism
As it mentions spring
Though it's gone too fast and here too soon
As it mutates to the charge
Of daily frustrations
Saturating the skin as it causes panic
I recall a place in time when that was me
I can still relate

The further I go the more I realize
There's no reason to sit idly by
Allowing life to exit my lungs
Before I've truly inhaled it

If given a choice
I'd carry love and triumph with me
And leave this wasted time behind

I Didn't Want To End Up Like You

Years of incessant transmissions
Calling for trees to topple over
Lives to balance on stilts
Hurling hatchets at rivals

I was shooting broken arrows
Wearing rusted armor
The flight was doomed from its origin
Long before I pressed the eject button

No lighting in a dark room
Microscopes are amassing dust
Tired of waiting for an encore
The spectators have left for home

My ship docks at sea
Still within the same sky
I breathe in the saline expansion
Somehow a prehistoric void is filled

A child shrouded in obscurity
Craving heroes over excuses
Annihilating fear of truth-telling
Because I didn't want to end up like you

She's Been Waiting

He dressed in new dancehall clothes
Even though it was unnecessary
The mirror approved and he floated on
A stop at the liquor store in town

Alone on arrival, he met her there
Fascinating specimen, the words in his mind
They spun and lifted, not missing any moments
At the end she left without good-bye

He pretended it didn't matter
As he always did before
Still it builds inside as impurity
One day there's no more room

The lights went out in the dance hall
The box was no match for his abrasive hands
The money felt strange in his grasp
Until he ran into cover of night

Placement can shape and destroy
When you can't see within, you're out
His advancements fell before him
She didn't approve of his methods

He didn't do what she'd asked
So she didn't give him a second chance
After he said he did it for her
Now he's alone without excuses

It doesn't feel like home
Somewhere is nowhere
Here he stays in denial of truths
Yielded by destructive patterns of fear

One morning a knock on the door
He ignored the urge to run
Opting to go willingly
A repeat offender
Now longing for accountability

Years later at the chamber
Their eyes lock at the luncheon
She looks away but cannot contain
She's been waiting

World Of Gigabytes

The moon hung low
I made my way to the sky
Assembling outside the atmosphere

There was no fashion
No channels
No speed of life
No deadlines

Shuffling through the electronic debris
Remaining in my head
To which I made claims
To never become accustomed
But I did

The stillness stinging the synapses
An overtone of stars wrapped in polyethylene

Dispose of feelings
Send arguments on hiatus
Another dreadful call to make
Generating shortness of breath
Endless disruptions
There is no outside
In the world of gigabytes

Playground

A wild man with a flat top
Preaches to the church choir
Like a firebug sucking out sin
With snakes in hand
The new way to believe he's right

The bus driver lets her hair down
As the snake man stands in rear view
Owls flutter wings at the door
While the phone continues ringing

Food is scarce on the playground
The bird's mind turns to cannibalism
The bushes are too thick to maneuver
His thoughts too slow to act

Forced to rely on the snake man
To feed the world and the fury
The gentleman cowers in the corner
Lighting his cigarette

Choking on the notes he's singing
Tripping on the chords he's playing
The cold seizes king flamboyance
As a crowd of people gather around

The gentleman is ancient history
The last will and testament is ignored
The perverted world laughs with insincerity
As the snake man takes the prize

Alone

If I dreamed I was standing over my grave
Would I be mournful?
What if I jumped off the wheel?
Would I spin out of control?

What if the mileage doesn't make the journey?
What if I became lost in familiarity?
Why does chaos and unrest come easy?
Does anyone recognize when I feel alone?

It's different for everyone
Can they know what it's like for me?
I can feel alone in moments, seconds
I can understand, then forget
I'm alone every day
The significance recurrently changes

Can they tell if it's never spoken?
Does it change like contagion?
If you find a happily ever after
Alone will find you again

Alter

A quarter century endured in wonder
Why my best wasn't good enough
Great days were neighboring catastrophe
Victories tied to disclaimers

It's hard to fight with little fight left
Late afternoon before I take flight
Idling requires a journey of one hundred miles
As failure follows close behind

I can't be a finished product
When chemicals are my co-pilot
Altering my brain
I don't know if my thoughts are my own

Difficulty in steadfastness
When I can't rely on myself
Fear of enduring a lifetime
In circular patterns unsustainable

I seek the heavens to find an approach
I seek the sunlight to alter my course
I look to these hands to climb ancient walls
That leave shadows cast over my life

I need to move on from the town of old
Take steps to be unabridged
So I can create distance from myself
To recondition the means of who I am

Grain Of Salt

At the corner of center and whirlwind
He tried to escape a vicious circle
Leaving it behind
Onto New Mexico
Tomorrow's word on the street
Three bullet holes through the windshield
Blood stains on the seat
Family knew of his struggles for a better life
That remained with him until the last day

I watch from the other side of the street
They don't care to know me
I'm conditioned to feel the same
I guess I do
Immersed in trivial disparities
Enough to consume my thoughts
I could let it roll off my back
If I took it with a grain of salt

Some things are better left unsaid
Instead of endeavoring to explain
In the end it only proves our point
I know you want to build
I know you want the earnings
As you close your eyes to voiced concerns
I mourn the death of common sense
On the initiation of declared change
Irony and red tape bring development to a halt
It'd be easy to point fingers and find fault
But I'll take it with a grain of salt

Proof

Shadows prove sunshine
In times when the unforeseen
Is nothing like you'd hoped
Exactly what you needed

Wisdom and suffering
Claims of apparitions
Flying objects and unknowns
Enough to fill a lifetime
If eyes remain open

Lightning and rain
An era of searching
Will end with hands empty
Unless you know it's always been there

Kindness and hope
Remain still and contemplative
Seek the sound of your breath
Love and belief will discover you
It should be the only proof you need

Overcome

Fields once vibrant
Now downtrodden and deserted
Under dim rolling vapors
Below the line of soldierly ambush
I was left discarded

When there are whispers of new discovery
I go where the work takes me
In a farmland of freedom and equivalence
There are faces born of acceptance
With eagerness to open their arms

Faith and trust in family
Leaves a voice and identity after fallouts
The blood in my veins is not a condemnation
If purified with honesty

I am not someone of war waging
Nor lost in an ocean of identity
The gates of this battered domain
Have been closed to further scrutiny

The foreign proposal of reorganization
Has a perpetual designation of prohibition
I have overcome the weights on my shoulders
While charting a course away from my history
These hands will go to work again

Moth Trapped In A Train Car

This day is a rapid heartbeat
A revolving door
I find myself uncollected
A rabid animal in a burned out building

Under the surface
This perfunctory dance of famine
My roots in need of water
Fluttering my wings across the ceiling
By the force of impact
I lose the way I'm headed
If I'm leaving or just arriving
A moth trapped in a train car

Today I gave it all
But I might be wrong
Spider webs in pavement
Roots breaking the surface
Grass growing in the cracks

I know you will see me again
In a different kind of light
You'll realize this day was the end
It was a long time coming

Like Ashes

Bells in the morning air
Arrivals acknowledge this departure
We leave our umbrellas in the antechamber
Reflection is a filthy secret

On a carousel of reminiscence
Substituted for present-day tragedy
These old photos smile back
Oblivious to current affairs

We fought outwardly, constantly
Though our battles were internal
We convinced ourselves there were no answers
So we scattered like ashes

Today we gather one last time
To honor a last request
Pay our grievances
Offer our reverence

A thoughtful homage and finale
Parting ways with the way it was
Saint Peter promised he would be there
So we shed our hope of reconciliation
And we scatter like ashes once again

Limitations

He opens his eyes from extended slumber
Originated in a simple world
Now complex as elevation
Deceiving as the sun in winter

After one hundred years of silence
Life channels through his veins
Like passing cars on paved streets
Among thoroughfares without limits

His descent is downward
Exposing all limitations
Like a rope slowly unraveling

Then she became the beacon
The reason he dreamt
A course official
His safety net

Then his ascent begins
A mind focused on nomadic feet
He abandons the lot

The storm damaged vital parts
Strewn rubble in its wake
The face in his dreams is unfazed
Waiting for him at the foothills

Through the cloak of limitations
She perceived integrity and truth
In a man who had to lose it all
To realize what was truly in his heart

Bird's Eye

A large portrait immersed in white
With a tiny spot of red
A cardinal looks down from a snowy branch
On a man with a shovel in hand
Digging out from a late winter storm

The bird's color is a flare
A beautiful accent to an already radiant scene
Where the calm and quiet of the day after
Shapes the setting for his next song

The cardinal fulfills his destiny
Perching in this bare tree
Remaining in this position
Watching this creature with such supremacy
Exhibit so much subordination and pain

He returns day after day
A ritual marked by the sun's position
Occasionally observing two of them
At times they carry on with raised voices
Other days emitting a glow so bright
As if their spring colors were on display
Singing new songs, varying their call signs

Never realizing
They don't need wings to fly
Nor dreams to live
They just need to see a challenge
For what it is and isn't
So they can arrive and maintain
And let the morning beckon the sun
As they rise on the spirit of the wind
Hear simplicity in the songs of birds
Adapt it as their life's motto
Arrive in the nest of the present
And remain there

Placeholder

I ran in between the lines
I thought the trial run was the race
The rehearsal a performance
A substitute the main character

Like bookends on a shelf
You were good with the edges
With a veil over your eyes
You could've been me

You were contoured and contrasted
I was pushed and pulled
Lead down a road
I thought I had chosen

You reigned the land
You knew your purpose
Cancelled the broadcast
So shame on you

I saw red flags
Yet refused to change course
I had been pardoned
In the end it was shame on me

If I had read the blue prints
I could've perceived your true motive
I was always just a placeholder
Never anything more

Typical

Something didn't feel right
When we stepped inside
I claimed I was misinformed
Actually I didn't listen

I told you this was the place
It must have been the other one
Your eyes tell me everything
You turn in disgust

Typical are my misjudgments
Continuously flying in enemy airspace
Falling off the tight rope
Losing sight of reality's symbols

On the road in the car
You in the passenger's seat
As your five miles away
Turned in the opposite direction

Rolling to a complete stop
The idle rattles unwarranted parts
The tension rattles my threadbare nerves
Only then do you let half a smile slip

The next day I get it right
I'm the difference between poles
It's surprising the drastic turn of events
You say there's still hope for me
Maybe someday

Devil's Tombstone

One flag has flown for centuries
The wind reminisces about another time
When the ship yards were abandoned
Flooded in a foundation of lies

Standing in formation
Soldiering trees line the roads
Their tops cut for wires

No thoughts escape me anymore
As if Mother Nature is a trustee
Either this or the end of belief
Of a city on the rise

I stare into the mid-day sun
I'm not sure how communication lines work
It's a lesson I had to learn
A test I had to pass

Past the park and pavilion lies an empty grave
Beneath the devil's tombstone
The earth's breath
Permeates the assembly of those trees
I hear the sound of steady waves
Echoes of children laughing
In the direction of the county line
I wrote the sky a letter
It was time to guide me home

Margaret The Beekeeper

Margaret left her home in Widlow
Pressing the pedal down slowly
Taking in the days for their worth
She knew she was a fortunate one

Her internal clock was slowing
Never frightened of her own demise
Only the wellbeing of her bees
That she served, protected, honored, and loved
Over a decade of communion
She was the balance in nature
A mother and messenger

The only day she didn't travel
Was the first day in a long time
A small service to follow
With friends and family
Acknowledging a humanitarian life

Shortly after the burial
It was said her bees made a journey
Several miles away from where she kept them
Assembling across the street from her home
They paid their respects, some say
To a woman who gave them everything
They lingered in remembrance for an hour
Then vanished over the rooftops

Grander Scheme Of Things

Beneath the rubble and ruins of this city
Lies a broken truce
Puzzle pieces of the past
Flags are tattered and torn
Historical remains sprinkled
Beneath wilted flowers

The pulse of the universe outside these walls
Echoes of footsoldiers' demise within
They wait for delivery of a new day's promise
Frozen in lines of darkness

One thousand fingers pointing
To a history of violated trust
The delirium that ignorance is bliss
Has burned beside opposing flags

They join the ranks of those in mourning
Holding the reigns of sleeping through life
Unable to get back in step
Beside canvasses of varying loyalties

In the grander scheme of things
My memory serves me too well about this
As the sun dances across the outer walls
Into to the great hall
A treaty ends the siege warfare
Still a quiet war wages on

Sticks And Stones

At the start of this journey
My heart was made of sticks and stones
Hallowed ground once filled with camaraderie
Where I claimed myself a visionary

Now solidified of bricks and mortar
A refuge for the fragile soul
The part that carries on
When the work here is done
I have a place carved out
I will exist here for a while
I will not hold onto impermanence

Losing time in footsteps
Seeking the enigmatic merchants of reform
Saying goodbye to loved ones
To those I once believed in
Who once believed in me
My field of vision is all I have
Gaining distance from my passage
Burning of all bridges that lead home

Trader

He leads an armada of knowledge
As a trader polishing his craft
He shaped the world as he wanted
The odds followed in his favor
Living by honorable principals
Taking no more than he was owed
Telegraphing his success
Through able bodied markets
As the pendulum begins to swing

He sifted through the spoils
While sitting on top of the world
But it wasn't long after
That the need for his resources dried up
They could've told him the truth
Or preached the gospel of his ego
Instead they built a story
From a mass of broken leaves
Within it a rise to prominence
Followed by a plummet of equal proportions
As the pendulum continues to swing

With no additional services to offer
He couldn't justify his marketability
Beginning to feel of little importance
Unable to fit into the holes carved out
From a detrimental force of rules
He stands on the frozen coastline
Depths below and sky above
Somewhere there are answers
Something is out there just for him
He hasn't given up
He feels it in his bones
The pendulum will swing his way again

Leave For The Moon

This place has changed
The sign reads *under new supervision*
Those we called friends are gone
On to better and bigger

Outside they're building subdivisions
Closing down streets
Their policies changed overnight
We have been waking up wondering

Once directing a gentle hand
The comfort of a warm embrace
Today there's an oppressive mindset
Weighing down the lines of communication

We've come a long way, but now it's just us
The love among and around has strained
We don't see who they are anymore
They don't see us

I know you nested here long ago
It feels like a welcome worn
Maybe an essential and much needed step
An eventual coming of age

The vitality of this arrival
Was inadequately anticipated
Forever may have arrived too quickly
It's time to leave for the moon

Attraction

If I weigh my importance
I receive a glance you'd never admit to
As you continue onward at your clip
Pretending to stay focused on the task at hand

If I say I'm in the game
If I act aloof enough
Giving signs of disinterest
Am I obeying the rules of attraction?

I've taken my earnings
I'm leaving the table
I need nothing more to survive

I celebrate every moment I see you
All others in between
No more smokescreens or playing roles
It's the end of giving part
And hiding the rest

This is the time to erase
The abolishment of facades
It's a time for following through

I paint with all of my colors
I operate at full power
If you motion I will deny
These laws of attraction no longer apply

San Damiano Interprovincial

I step onto these grounds to say my piece
But a deafening silence slows my pace
The occupation of words
Previously infiltrating my mind
Abandoned in the rustle of foliage
In the arcs of limestone shelters

I push the door open
Unknowing what I would find
I was graced by antiquity in song
A choir in praise of twin pillars

Sunlight in lavender
Through stained glass
The energy drew me in
Faith in abundant display
Yet not in broadcast
I wonder why I had to travel so far to find

Time was fleeting as I absorbed the fallow
With an engaged heart I set off
Part of my spirit adhered to the mortar cracks
Lying inside the reason for its existence

Universal history of echoes
In the crunching of leaves underfoot
Culture changing in the windmills of time
Still in some way it has remained the same

To Distinction

All these accolades
For showing a side of yourself
That under any other circumstances
Would cause embarrassment and heartache
Apparently it's good to be dissident
It's popular to be short of straws
To be the man that does all of the things
That no woman wants a man to do

Still your popularity exceeds this commitment
Here you are giving advice
Writing memoirs, winning hearts
Basking in the sun by the ocean
On the deck of the beach house you now own
While the many who never sold their soul
Look at you with anger and envy
Wondering if they should change their values
So they can find a way to get ahead

You make it look so easy
Being cheap and easy
Leave it to us to feed your ego
As we roll out the red carpet for you
Welcome to distinction for doing nothing

The Next Frame

Winds over the crest of the hill
Martial law of a new season approaches
Decolonization of the tired replacement
To recover from the abuse of encounters

Disputes over trade and territory
Secret ballots for self-denying ordinances
Battling for positioning in spaces
Mandates for sheltering from cold posterity
I am always anticipating the next frame
In a feature with limited showings

A society for the reformation of manners
Argues coins and currency in coffee houses
I leap into skies from mountains
Gambling on the surety of safe landings
Expectations of a home coming parade
When I've only been a no-show

Secularism in a silent spring
The surrounding boroughs exercise resistance
I was told to follow my heart
Wherever it leads me
For what one gives away with true compassion
In the final frame will be refunded
With compound interest

Birds Of Siberia

Passive Sun
Queen of ice in mortal form
Settling the score

This mission
Find my frozen, buried soul
Before it's too late

Simple fear
Prevents this exploration
Exoneration

Playful heart
Ravens rolling in the snow
The joy of living

Spread your wings
The birds of Siberia
Feel warmth inside cold

Sunrise

A diurnal tradition
Where it begins and ends
Stillness in between moments
The thoughts of a reflecting world

Every time could be the first time
The novelty of salvation is attained
Arms are wide to an embrace
To feel greatness of moments in rebirth

Calmness in gratitude of anticipation
Gazing through windows of our universe
Minds as still as the depths of space
Focus as fragile as a single fallen leaf

One day can be a lifetime
Enduring to elude our thoughts
We risk forgetting magnificence all around
When we move too quickly

This communion will release the spirit
Ready to rejoice with another presentation
Appreciation of incremental importance
As we awaken in tribute once again

If I Could

I would appoint you the queen of sleeping
There wouldn't be a day you didn't get enough
You'd never worry about time wasted
Doing something you didn't love
You wouldn't have to be afraid
Of hardships or unfairness
Hidden in the cards we've been dealt

I would give you every opportunity to breathe
Make you as happy as I am able
Give you everything you wanted
Be everything you need
So there would be no reason to dream
If I could

Of A Feather

Waiting here in the north
For introduction to the south
Create a ripple in the sky
We move among the treetops
As we wait for our summoning

This dawn lends us light
We have known this medieval way
Now we feel it in our bones again
As if it's guiding us remotely

If you knew me for one thousand years
This would be my unfading song and color
As goes my fearlessness
You would still be the one
We will always be birds of a feather

In A Moment

I stepped outside
Inhaled the quiet
From the overturned internal world
Looking up was looking down

I found calm in chaos
The exhale of the earth was peaceful
It was only a moment in a lifetime
Everything will be alright
Everything will work itself out

Dearly Departed

Early Sunday morning
The helicopter comes to take her away
In the wisdom of the moment
I fail to find passage

Perpetual are the peaks and the valleys
Forming patterns like rain down windows
Every time it ends the same
As it begins again

To the dearly departed
A demise eternally imbalanced and unfair
Pain lies in reminiscence
To bury the past even more so

The hearts will still be attached
The eyes that watched can't forgive
The dearly departed will forever be missed
Within us they will always live

One Truth

In an empty field of green
A crowd begins to gather
It's been a long time coming
This journey of acceptance

Acceptance that there are few answers
That there will be sunshine and storms
Droughts and floods
Acceptance that we must endure
Together, not apart

We are far from battle
Far from the need to cry
From the need to exhume and overanalyze
Our past crimes against one another

The borders do not bring comfort
If not for a sliver of light in open space
At the roots, one hope
Love

Love
A monolithic force
Casting shadows on desolation and sorrow
A constant among variables
Decommissioning animosity
An undeniable doctrine
Building empires of faith
Giving into you when you give into it
Our one hope of existence
One truth
Love

Thank you

www.ingramcontent.com/pod-product-compliance
Lightning Source LLC
LaVergne TN
LVHW050941080826
845145LV00004B/1359

* 9 7 8 0 6 1 5 7 7 3 9 0 2 *